Cricut Project

Ideas 2

More Cutting Designs and Patterns That Will Spark Creativity

Michelle L. Fischer

Table of Contents

Introduction

What You Can Expect to Learn In this Book

The purpose of this book is to inspire the creative crafter in you through your Cricut machine. You might have been gifted this machine, or you might have picked one up at your art supply store. You might be thinking to yourself, *okay I have this machine, but now, what exactly can I make or do with a Cricut*? Well, this will be the book that will answer the majority of your questions that you may have when you are first starting out.

Within this book, I broke down the chapters, with the first two being for those who want to know exactly what they will need, in order to begin using their Cricut machine. If you consider yourself somewhat familiar with the concept, and would like to read through different project ideas, then feel free to skip over to the third chapter. However, within these first two chapters, you will learn what tools you will need to invest in to make your crafting as easy and simple as possible. You will also learn about the different materials that you can invest in, depending on what kind of projects you plan to take on.

I understand that learning how to use a new piece of technology can be challenging and often frustrating, which was what inspired me to write this book: To help you guys learn. Within the projects that you will read about, I did my best to try and explain the process of completing the project, as well as tips and tricks that you could implement to make the process a lot easier. If you can accept that there will be a lot of trial and error, especially for those of you who are barely starting, you will come to realize how rewarding it is to be able to create your custom crafts. The beauty of this book is that it will help prepare you for what you need, as well as provide you with my own experience with working with my Cricut machine for over seven years.

I have several friends who have mastered the use of their Cricut machine, and have even started using their Cricut as a way to bring in extra income. Many of the projects that will be discussed in this book can be made and sold, given the right market demand. Even if you're skimming through this book, I encourage you to take a look at each chapter and see what sparks your creative imagination.

Materials 101: Items You Will Need for Your Cricut Machine

For those of you who may have been recently gifted a Cricut machine, or for those of you who have had a Cricut, but never really knew exactly what kind of materials you needed, this is a perfect run-through of some of the essentials that you may need to take on some of the projects that you will be reading on in this book. I get it, when I first got my Cricut, I was a bit overwhelmed. I had gone to Michaels and Hobby Lobby thousands of times because I didn't know what I was doing, or what I needed to buy. I don't want you guys to be discouraged by feeling lost, or to keep buying things you don't need, or missing things that you need. I thought it would be so helpful to do a quick run-through of some important items.

One of the first investments is getting a basic starter toolset. Your basic toolset will come with a scraper that is used to scrape and flatten your vinyl or card material onto your mat. The more projects you begin to take, the more you will see how important having a scraper is, to ensure that what you are working with sticks onto your mat. The next item is your weeding tool. Your weeding tool will become your best friend, because nearly every project requires some form of weeding. Your basic toolset will most likely come with a spatula, tweezers, a scoring tool, and, sometimes, a cute little pair of scissors. I would still invest in a good pair of scissors that will last you a long time because you will be cutting a lot, depending on the types of projects you do. For the most part, you can find these starter toolsets at Michaels,

Hobby Lobby, or you can even order them on Amazon. These tools alone will easily allow you to complete many of the projects that you may take on.

Some other fun items to have are Cricut pens, which your new machine will come with some already, but you can buy different pens that will change the line patterns. For example, you can get a pen with a marker tip, or a pen with a finer tip. But you don't need these pens unless you are going to be experimenting with the writing function, because the pen that the machine comes with will do just fine.

Other things that you will want to invest in are mats. They come in three different grip strengths. The light blue mat is the light grip mat, and this is the mat that I would recommend getting, because it will be the most-used mat. You are going to want to use this mat when you are working with vinyl, cardstock, paper, or anything lightweight. Then, you have the green mat, which is your standard grip mat. I will use this mat from time to time, but not as much as the blue mat. The green mat will just provide extra hold that may not be necessary all the time. Lastly, you have the purple mat, which is your heavy-duty grip mat. This is the mat that will be needed the least, unless you are working with fabrics or anything heavy. For example, the one time that I used my purple mat was when I made my own Halloween costume, because the material I was using was felt. Sometimes, you can find these mats sold in a variety pack. That way, you have different grip strengths for different projects that you might work on. If you want to take it up a notch, you can invest in big mats, which are 12 x 24, which will provide you with ample space for bigger designs. I enjoy working on a bigger mat, because I won't feel limited in regards to space, which allows me to play around with different designs while I am brainstorming my ideas.

The next items that you will be needing will be based on what you would like to use your Cricut for. Don't worry if you don't have a clue on what you plan on doing with your Cricut; I will run through some of the materials you might be interested in, and what they can be used for. I very much enjoy working and cutting vinyl with my Cricut machine. Vinyl can be cut and used on: Glasses, cups, and cell phone cases, just to name a few. There are two types of vinyl: One being permanent, and the other type of vinyl is not permanent. I would recommend investing in heat transfer vinyl (HTV) if you are planning on working with transferring designs onto clothes. I purchase my HTV from 6 v 1 vinyl—they have amazing customer service, and they also ship your purchases very fast.

Another item that you may want to invest in, is cardstock. On cricut.com, they have a ton of samplers, and with the season approaching, you can look through different fall samples. There are countless color options to choose from. Other items you might consider investing in are different colored paints if you plan on painting on items such as wood to make custom signs. Paint brushes, such as a foam brush or thin brushes can be used for touch-ups. I would suggest buying a variety pack of brushes, because they will always come in handy when doing any kind of painting project.

Again, these are just some of the basic tools as well as materials that will get you started on using your Cricut machine. I strongly encourage you to continue reading on to see what project ideas might interest you, so that you will know exactly what materials you would like to buy first.

Tips and Tricks for Cricut Newbies

Although for each project I will be giving some tips and tricks, I thought it would be nice to have one portion of the book dedicated to showing some basic tips and tricks for those of you who may be new to the Cricut machine, or for those of you who might need a refresher.

I understand that when you first begin using your Cricut machine, it might be overwhelming, and you might be thinking that you won't ever learn how to use it. But just before you store your Cricut away in the garage, never to see the light of day, I urge you to continue reading to learn some very simple and easy tricks that will help spark the inner crafter in you.

The first tip that I would like to share with you all is that there will be a learning curve when first starting out using the Cricut machine. Before that turns you off of learning, please understand that, with every new piece of technology that you are introduced to, it may take some time before you figure it out. But the most rewarding part of the process is that, when you learn how to operate this new piece of technology, that is when your crafting possibilities will become endless.

One of the neatest things about learning something new these days is that we all, for the most part, have access to the Internet. One of the most beneficial resources I had that taught me how to operate my Cricut machine was the YouTube videos posted by fellow crafters like myself. Nothing beats watching the process of someone crafting something. Even if you have no intention of crafting what is being made on the YouTube videos, you can see how they are operating their Cricut machine. Many of the projects that you might take on will follow similar steps or the same process of operating your circuit. I strongly encourage you to begin watching YouTube videos, because many of your readers might be visual learners.

I would strongly suggest getting connected with fellow crafters. Facebook has tons of groups that can give insight and help over social media. You may also draw inspiration or ideas from what your fellow crafters might be making.

The second tip that I have for you all is to get accustomed to the Cricut language. For example, you might hear some videos where crafters refer to "HTV", "six five one", or "six three one", and for someone new, you might be thinking that they're speaking in a new language. For this reason, in this book, if I refer to "HTV", it means "heat transfer vinyl" in long form. The nice thing is that we all have Google at our fingertips. If or for some reason, an acronym or piece of material is not explained, we can easily look up the meaning. You may hear terms such as "weld" and "attached". Although they may seem as though they are doing the same thing, they perform different tasks. "Welding" is essentially attaching everything, but it will get rid of the overlapping lines. You will want to use this when you're trying to merge a project into shapes. This is a small example, but it goes to show how terms will become beneficial in the learning process, because when time comes to applying the term to your project, you will either know how to do it, or know how to ask for help using the proper terminology.

My third tip, for you crafters, is to find your nearest dollar store. You will soon learn to love and appreciate the dollar store when you begin crafting. There are so many useful items that you can buy in bulk or experiment with at the dollar store. Especially if you are just starting out, the dollar store will be perfect for buying blank coffee mugs, wine glasses, plates, and simple items that you can turn into your piece of art.

My fourth tip, when working with heat transfer vinyl, is to mirror your image. This was probably the most frustrating thing that I dealt with when I began experimenting with heat transfer vinyl. What happened to me is that I would have my design all cut out and ready to transfer onto my shirt, but the problem being that, if I did not mirror my image when cutting out the design, I would end up transferring my image onto my shirt backward. If you forget to mirror your heat transfer vinyl and you don't turn it shiny-side down, you will have wasted all of your HTV. After reading all of the tips and tricks, I would say that this tip will save you lots of money, because you will not be wasting your HTV on a simple mistake that can be avoided. The only exception will be for printable HTV: You do not have to mirror your image, but when you begin the cutting process, you'll need to make sure that you are cutting your design with the image facing up.

Tip number five: I encourage you to save your scraps. You might be thinking that, once you trim or cut pieces off of your stencils, that the pieces you cut out are trash, but they can still be useful. I keep a bag of my scraps, which contains different color vinyls that I've worked on—different color card stocks. There are countless colors and sizes of scraps that can be beneficial for future projects. You never know when you might need a small square of glitter HTV.

Tip number 6, would have to be investing in storage containers to make sure that all your Cricut tools and accessories are safe and easy to locate area. Once you begin taking your crafting to the next level, I would urge you to create a small space, with maybe a work desk, so that you can have one area dedicated to your crafts. The last thing that you would want to happen is that, while you are working on your craft, all of a sudden you need your weeding tool or scraper, but you can't find it. One of the most frustrating things is not knowing where you put something. I urge you to try and stay as organized as possible, because this will save you a lot of time and frustration.

My last tip before we begin diving into some awesome crafting projects, is to be kind to yourself. Something that I learned through the process is that crafting is a marathon, and not a sprint. Enjoy the process, and just try to have fun with it. As you get better at crafting, it might become something that you do to make extra income by selling some of the stuff that you make, but just remember to enjoy what you are creating. There is going to be a lot of trial and error, but it will all be worth it in the end, when you're able to gift that special someone something that you took the time to create. The sentimental value attached to that piece of art is priceless. So, let's get started on some simple ideas that you can begin experimenting with.

Life is so much easier when we know our way around. Any piece of information that will help us will go a long way, which is why I thought it would be important to have a small portion dedicated to some hacks that will take your Cricut crafting skills to the next level.

The more you begin to use your Cricut, the more you realize how important your mat is. With that being said, the first three hacks will involve your Cricut mats.

I'm sure you are aware that all your mats come with a plastic film that covers the adhesive side of your mat—I like to call this my "dust cover". The problem that I've experienced over my years of using the Cricut machine is figuring out what side is the right side to put the plastic back on my mat. When you remove the plastic covering, you will notice that it is a bit sticky due to your mat. The problem is that, if dust or debris gets onto this plastic when you put the plastic back on your mat, all that dust and debris will have now transferred onto your mat.

So, you have to make sure that, when you remove your dust cover, that you put it in a safe location where unwanted debris will not be collected. The other issue that happens is when you place the dust cover on the opposite side. When you do this, there is more of a chance of having dust and debris collected on your dust cover. So, the next time you use it, if you end up flipping your dust cover back to the original side, all the debris that was collected will be transferred onto your mat. For this reason, I like to place a small sticker on the top side of my dust cover—this reminds me of what side is the correct side that faces up.

Another thing that I like to do on my mats is to mark the date in which I start using my mat. This date will give me a rough idea of how long my mats are lasting. You will learn that there are going to be certain mats that you will need to buy more of, because the projects that you are doing use a specific kind of mat. You might be thinking why this is helpful to know? Well, when a big sale comes along, you will know exactly what kind of mats you need to buy— possibly in bulk. For example, on Black Friday, some stores will have mats at fifty percent off. Knowing roughly how long my mats last me, I was able to buy six months' worth of mats at fifty percent off the price. If you don't know how long your mats are lasting, chances are, you might be overspending, or not buying mats at the right time, which is why dating your mats is so easy and simple. In the long run, this habit will save you lots of money.

I would suggest investing in some 3M hooks for your dust covers. Often, you may come to find out that your dust covers are one of the items that you tend to misplace by accident. You're finally done using your mat, and you can't find your cover? I like these 3M hooks because I can hang my dust covers in a spot where I know for sure they will be.

The last hack that I have for your mats, especially if you have a mat that is getting a little old, and the sticky part of the mat is lacking on the amount of hold that you need, you can use wide, blue, painter's tape. The painter's tape will hold down whatever material that you are going to be cutting. That way, the blade on your machine won't be pushing your material around. Wide blue painter's tape also comes in handy when you are weeding and working on vinyl. What I like to do is wrap some of the blue painter's tape, with the sticky side facing out, around my fingers. As you are weeding, whatever pieces that are being weeded out can be placed onto your sticky hand. That way, you are collecting all of the trash.

The next hack will allow you to make sure that your blades are the right sharpness for the project that you will be working on. What I have started to do over the years is keep two extra blades in my storage compartment in my Cricut machine. I then mark the plastic that covers the blade with a letter signifying what that blade is specifically for. For example, if I am going to be cutting glitter paper, you will notice that the sharpness of your blade runs out a lot faster. For this reason, I like to cut with the same blade marked for glitter, so that I know roughly how many cuts a blade can give me when cutting glitter paper. I will also have a blade for cutting vinyl to kind of have the same estimate. I noticed that having specific blades assigned for different materials has helped me preserve the longevity of my blades, which, in turn, has saved me money.

The last hack, which I found to be fascinating, is that you can use Crayola markers in "Clamp A" as your pens for writing with your Cricut machine. This is an awesome hack that I had ran into on YouTube. A perfect alternative to using styling pens if you already have these markers at home. That way, you have one less thing that you have to invest in. But please be warned that Cricut does not recommend doing this, and if you would like, Cricut sells their styling pens.

I thought it would be nice to just have these tips and tricks, because they might come in handy as you begin working with your Cricut machine more and more.

How to Make an Iron-On Design for Your T-Shirt with Cricut Using Heat Transfer Vinyl (HTV)

I enjoy this project because it is so much fun to create custom designs on, and being able to wear them. I usually will go on to Amazon.com and purchase in bulk different colored plain t-shirts, so that I can place my design on different color t-shirts, or make several shirts with different designs.

This project can be very useful if you're planning on making team t-shirts for your son or daughter's baseball and softball teams. Or, maybe, if you have an upcoming family reunion, this will be a perfect way to have all of the family in their custom shirts with their names on it.

To get started, there will be the following items that you will need. To start with, you will need a t-shirt or some form of apparel that you will be ironing the design onto. You will also need the heat transfer vinyl (HTV) and the colors that you wish to use. A cutting machine—in our case, the Cricut—along with Cricut Design Space, which is an app that lets you design and wirelessly cut with Cricut Explore and other Cricut machines will be needed. You will also need an iron and preferably an ironing board to evenly iron out the design. If you have all of these items on hand, then we can get started.

The first step in this process is figuring out what you would like to design. It could be anything, such as an image of your favorite band or sports team, or any kind of writing or font style that you like. After selecting an image, you will then upload this image onto your design space through your computer.

After the image has been uploaded onto your design space, you're going to resize the image to the desired size that you would like on your t-shirt. For example, if you are going to be designing a small t-shirt with a company logo, you can go with the dimensions of 8 in width, and just about 2 in height.

When you are done with the design, you will then go to the upper right-hand corner, and click the green "make it" button, which will then take you to the next screen. On this screen, you will be able to see exactly how your HTV needs to be positioned on your Cricut map to cut the full image. One important thing to remember, when working on any HTV project, is to select the mirror for the iron-on button. This option flips the numbers, so, in that way, you won't iron-on your image backwards. After doing so, you will go to the bottom right-hand corner and click "continue."

At this point, you will need your Cricut map and your HTV, and you will need to place the design where it needs to go. For example, if you will be using two different colors, you will need to position your design where they need to be once the image is mirrored. You may notice that there is a white backside and a clear backside on your HTV. It is important to note that the clear plastic side is the side that will be going face-down.

Once your HTV is on your map and secured in place, you're going to want to make sure that you set the dial on your Cricut to "iron-on". To load your machine, take your map, holding it flush to the bar, and then hit the blinking button. The machine will then begin to adjust itself, and the Cricut button will begin to flash. After pressing this button, the Cricut will begin to cut out your design.

When your machine has completed the cutout, you will press the flashing button to release the map from the Cricut. You will need a weeding tool—this tool will allow you to remove the excess vinyl that needs to be cut out from your design. When the mat has been removed from the Cricut, you will peel the HTV off of the map and begin weeding. You will notice that, when you are weeding and pulling off the extra vinyl material, the clear plastic backing will stay in place. When you are done, you will peel the design off of the map. After the design has been fully weeded, you will move on to the next step.

The next step in the process is to prep the shirt that you will be transferring your design onto. You will need your iron and a flat surface to ensure that your shirt is wrinkle-free where the design will be placed. A useful tip to ensure that your design is being placed perfectly centered, is to use a piece of chalk and a ruler. You will then measure and mark a center line going down from the collar, and a second line going across the shirt in your desired location.

You must have your iron settings set to a "no-steam" setting. With the iron nice and warm, and your t-shirt in place, you will then place your design, with the sticky side down, and using the graph, along with the lines that you marked on your shirt, in your desired location. Press your design down onto the shirt to ensure that it is has been securely placed.

You will then need a white cloth, or even a white pillowcase, which you will use in the ironing process. Place the white cloth or the pillowcase over the design. Next, grab your iron and begin applying pressure onto the cloth, moving the iron around, as if you were ironing a shirt. The process of ironing and transferring your design onto the shirt will take approximately thirty to forty-five seconds, depending on how thin or thick the lines are in your design. Another factor that affects how long the process of transferring the design onto your shirt will take, is how much pressure you are applying using the iron. Interestingly enough, thinner lines will take a bit longer to iron on than thicker lines. This is something to keep in mind during the ironing process.

When you feel as though you have ironed enough, you will then pull the white cloth off of your design. You will then begin to slowly peel around the edges of your design. Doing so, you will be able to see whether you need to iron on your design a bit longer, or if your design has already been fastened well onto the t-shirt. You will continue to peel at an angle, and, if, for some reason, you are finding that certain areas are sticking to the t-shirt, you can give the design a couple more passes with the iron. This will allow you to begin removing the vinyl more easily from the t-shirt.

After removing the plastic sheet from the t-shirt, place your white cloth back onto the t-shirt and begin ironing for another ten to fifteen seconds. This will ensure that your design has been securely transferred onto the t-shirt. After this step, you are all set to wash and wear your custom design t-shirt.

How to Make a Home Décor Sign: Vinyl Stencil on Wood

I'm sure on your trips to Hobby Lobby or Michael's, you've seen these cute wooden pieces that read "love" or "beautiful" in a fancy font, as if they were hand-painted. These home décor signs can be quite pricey at times. That's why, in this project, you will learn how to make your signs with your custom message that you would like displayed.

All you need is any flat piece of reclaimed wood, or store-bought wood. I prefer the rustic design, which is why I love to use reclaimed wood, which can come from an old wooden fence or a pallet. This type of wood will have a different texture, and will give your design piece more character. Important to note: You'll need to sand your piece of wood before you paint it. This will ensure that, when you transfer your design onto the wood, it will stick and come out clean. If you have a newly-bought piece of wood, you will want to sand it, and you can also stain the wood at this point. If you do decide to stain your piece of wood, it's a good idea to grab a paper towel and wipe off any of the excess staining to ensure that an even coat has been applied to it. You will also need to get some tape, acrylic paint, and paintbrushes. I recommend having a variety of paint brushes, depending on the type of lettering and design that you have.

Now that you have your piece of wood, you need to go onto your design space and select the image font that you would like to use on your piece of wood. When you have the image in your design space, you are going to want to re-size the image to the appropriate size of your wood. Once you have the font re-sized, you can then go to the top right-hand corner and click "make it."

Once you have the design made out, you will be able to run it through your Cricut machine to begin the cutting process. After your stencil has been cut, you will then need to cut out a piece of the transfer tape to fit the size of your stencil. You may then peel the transfer tape off, and place the sticky part of the tape onto your stencil. It's important to make sure that the tape is placed precisely over the stencil, and is then swooped to completely flatten the tape over the stencil. A good technique to use when swooping the tape onto your design, is to start in the middle of your design, and begin working your way out. This technique is quite similar to placing the protective screen on a touch-screen phone. With your scissors handy, you will trim any of the excess vinyl that may be hanging on your design.

Next, you will peel off the transfer, and the vinyl stencil should begin to stick onto the transfer tape. Try not to get frustrated if you begin to struggle to get your stencil to stick with the tape. Just take the process slowly, and enjoy the process.

After your design has been transferred onto the tape, you will then need to measure and see exactly where you would like your design to be placed on the wood. It's nice if you have a measuring tape or a ruler to measure exactly where the center is, so as to place your design, but they are not required. You can also use a ruler to mark any lines that may help you position your design.

Now that you have the design where you want it, you can begin to smooth it down onto the wood. This step is similar to the first step of placing the tape onto your design. My advice would be to start in the middle and begin smoothing it out in an outward motion. What you want to try and do is get rid of any of the air bubbles that you might see while it is under the transfer tape. Do not try to rush through this step; please take as much time necessary to fully smoothen out the design onto the wood.

After the design seems fully secured onto the wood and you have gotten rid of the air bubbles that may have appeared, you can then begin to peel the transfer tape off of your stencil. For this step, you don't want to remove the tape at a very slow pace, but you also don't want to rip the tape off either. You want to have a consistent peel, making sure that your stencil has fully settled onto the wood. For precautionary measures, you can smoothen the stencil onto the wood a second time. Be very careful doing so, as the transfer tape has already been removed, and you can easily damage or ruin the design by snagging a piece off of your stencil.

Now, the fun part begins, which is the painting portion of this project. You can use some of the scrap paper that you had from your stencil to place some paint on there. The paint I would recommend is the Artist Loft acrylic paint. The reason being that this paint has worked well for many of my past projects. Using this paint, I have noticed that I only need to go over my stencil with one to two passes of paint. I would recommend using a dry foam brush. For the first coat of paint, you don't want to drench your brush in paint, because what you are trying to do is lightly coat it. Begin painting with even strokes, going across and over the stencil. Don't worry if there are any letters that you feel are too light, because you will be going over the design again. An important rule of thumb for any painting project is to always start light because you can always add more paint, but it's hard to remove too much paint that has already been brushed in.

Once you have added as much paint as you would like to your piece of wood, you are then ready to peel the stencil off of the wood. Peeling the stencil off while the paint is still fresh is important because, if the paint dries too much, you risk peeling off the pain while removing the stencil. You will begin by peeling one corner of the stencil and gently begin peeling the stencil off. Don't worry if your stencil rips; at this stage of the project you do not need the stencil anymore. You may notice that there are still pieces of vinyl that may not have come off, so, at this point, you will be able to use your weeding tool to gently pick out these pieces of vinyl. After completing this process, your piece is complete and ready to be placed somewhere in your house.

How to Transfer Your Design Onto your Coffee Mug.

Nothing beats a nice warm cup of coffee to start off your morning right. It's rare to find someone who does not drink coffee, which is why a coffee mug is always a safe, affordable, and thoughtful gift to give to just about anyone. Which is why you will be designing your very own custom coffee mugs to give out to your friends and family for the holiday season.

The materials that you will be needing are: A big coffee mug—any color will just about do. You will also need some kind of permanent vinyl—any brand will work just fine. The one I typically use is 651 oracle vinyl by Oracles. You will also need a transfer tape.

So, for this project, we will be turning our basic white coffee mug into an artful mug with a cute message. If you don't have any cute fonts, I recommend you check out font bundles. You can write a cute message or something funny— the options are endless. Whatever color you would like your font to be in, you will need to make sure that the vinyl color is permanent.

You will cut out a piece of vinyl—roughly the length of the coffee mug's circumference. You will then place this vinyl sheet onto your mat, and begin scraping it as if you were placing a screen protector on your phone.

On your Cricut machine, you will have the settings set to your basic vinyl cutting setting. After doing so, present your mat to your Cricut machine, and begin the cutting process of whatever message you would like displayed on your coffee mug. When your Cricut has completed cutting out your design, you can remove the mat. Remove the design from your mat, and begin to weed out the extra vinyl that is around your lettering design. While performing this step, be gentle, so as to not damage or rip off any of the letterings that you will be using.

Now, we are on the easy part, and that is cutting out the transfer tape to begin placing our font onto the coffee mug. Place the transfer tape over the lettering and begin to scrape over the transfer tape to try and get the letters to stick on well. Once your font has been transferred onto your transfer tape, you will need to pick the side that you would like your design to be placed on your coffee mug. Do your best to try and center the font onto the mug. Begin by pressing the middle part down first, and then moving on to the sides and pressing down firmly. Once you have your design pressed onto your mug, you can give it a couple of scrapes to ensure that it is stuck on well.

Slowly begin to peel the transfer tape off, making sure that each letter has been transferred onto the mug and is not peeling off. A good technique to use is to press down on the transfer tape and begin peeling it back, while continuing to press down. There you have it: Your design has been successfully transferred onto your mug.

An important thing to keep in mind is that, if you choose a delicate font, it may not stand the test of time, and eventually, the lettering will begin to peel off. If the mug you are working on is for someone else, or if you're planning on selling the mug, I would suggest going for a robust font. However, if this mug is for your personal use, you can go with just about any font you wish. When working with vinyl on mugs or even wine glasses, the chunkier and bigger the design, the better the chance that the design will stay on. So long as you take care of the mug by not putting the mug in the dishwasher, soaking the mug in the sink, or placing the mug in the microwave, your mug design will last. When washing the mug, make sure to gently hand wash it.

This will be the perfect gift for just about anyone, or you can even use these as centerpieces at your next birthday party or bridal shower.

How to Make a Greeting Card or Birthday Card

We have all been on the receiving end a card, whether it has been for your birthday, Valentine's day, or even just a simple greeting card. It's nice to receive these types of cards because it shows you just how much someone thought of you, to get you a card, and write some sweet words inside it for you to read. This is why I love to make cards for any occasion, because it is so easy and affordable to make, and it brings me so much joy just being able to see the smiles I can get from my loved ones when they open up a personally-made card.

The materials that you will need to make a card is some card stock. Depending on how many colors you would like in your card, it will determine how many different card stocks that you will need to buy. You will need your mat to place your design to cut on your Cricut. You are also going to need a glue stick, or you can use glue dots if you want to keep it clean. You will need a scraper, or what others may call a "squeegee".

For this project, you will be working off of Design Space, which is the app I prefer to do my work on, since I am familiar with this program.

I typically like to make my cards 5 x 5, which is the conventional size for any card somewhat of a square shape. To start our card, you will head over to "Shapes" and select the square. To make a 5 x 5 card, the dimensions that you will need to make your square is 10 x 5, which is 10 inches wide and 5 inches long. The reason you are making the card a 10 x 5, is that the card will be folded in the center, which will make your card a 5 x 5 card. After you have the dimensions down, you will change the color of your rectangle to white, so you can see exactly what you are doing on the card.

Since the card will be folded in half, what you can do is click on "Shapes" and add a score line in the center of your card. What this score line does is that it tells the machine that you will be folding the card where the score has been placed, and the machine will make a perfect fold for you. You will place this score line on the 5, going vertically. Now, you need to attach the score line to the card. Click on the score line that you just placed on the card and hold down your "shift" key, and select the rectangle card, and click "attach" on the bottom right of your screen. Your score line will now be attached to your card, and you can begin the designing process.

Looking on your screen, the square on the right will be the front side of the card, and the left square will be on the back side of the card. If you would like your card to be two colors, for example, white and blue, what you will want to do is duplicate the rectangle that you made. To duplicate the rectangle, select the rectangle that you have made, and go to the right-hand corner and select "duplicate". A second rectangle will appear. You can then move this rectangle below the first one that you had. Now, for the second rectangle that you made, the square on the right side will be at the back of the front side of the card, and the left square will be at the front of the back of the card. Before moving on, you can change the color of any of the rectangles at this time.

To begin writing on the front of your card, you will select the "text" tool on the left side of your toolbar. On the top left, you can click on "font", and scroll through different fonts to find the font that you like the best. If you are using the pen feature on your Cricut, you are going to want to filter writing fonts and select from one of the fonts listed. Filtering out the writing fonts will give you the fonts that are meant to be used with the Cricut pen. Once you have found a font that you like, you will begin to type whatever you want to say at the front of your card. For example, if you are making a Valentine's day card, you can type in "I love you." After typing your message, you are going to want to center the writing. You will then resize the writing until it fits the way you would like on the front of your card. Before moving on, you'll need to change your setting on the right side under the text. You'll need to change it from the cutting symbol to the writing symbol.

If you would like to add images to your card, select the "image" tool on the left side of your screen. You may then search whatever images you would like on the top right corner. For example, sticking with the Valentine's theme, you can type in "flower bouquet". Some options will be free with your subscription, while others will require a small fee. When you select an image, on the right side, you will be able to see if it is compatible with card stock, because you will be able to see all of the layers. You will then be able to resize your image to your desired size. If, for some reason, you do not like the colors that were included in your image, you can change these colors at this time. To change the colors, on the right side of your screen, you can see the various layers of your image and the colors that have been designated to each part of the image. You can then click on the colors that you would like to change, and then select the colors that you would like to use instead.

Once you have changed the colors, or have selected the image that you wish to use, move the image over to the side for just a few moments. You will then select the card, as well as a highlight over the writing that you have placed on the front of your card. You will then click "attach" located on the bottom right corner. This will attach the writing onto your card, which will tell your Cricut machine that you want this writing to be written on the card. After doing so, you may then move the image back onto the front of your card. If you see that your image disappears when you are placing the image back on the card, you simply need to right-click on the image and click "move to the front".

If you would like your card to have some sort of a border, you can place the first rectangle that you are working on over the other card, and slightly shrink down the top rectangle. Your machine will then cut out both rectangles at different sizes, and when you get to the gluing stage, you will then be able to paste the cards onto one another in the same fashion that you had them on Design Space.

For the writing on the inside of your card, you can either hand write what you are going to say, or you can type in your message. I like to write my message inside of the card, but you can do either, or both. To write something inside of your card, you will follow the same steps that you did previously. Once all of your writing is attached to both the inside card and the outside part of the card, you can then turn on your machine and select "make it".

We will now be selecting our materials, which will be light card stock. We're going to watch to make sure that we load all of our tools, which includes our pen, and scoring wheel. If you have an Air two or an older model, you can just use the scoring stylist. If you have a scoring wheel, when that is fastened onto your Cricut machine, your machine will know that you want your card to be scored. At this point, you will also fasten your Cricut pen onto the machine. Make sure that the pen clicks in, as this will ensure that the pen has been securely fastened.

Grab your mat, as well as your card stock, and begin scraping it flat onto your mat with your scraper or squeegee. Once your card stock is on your mat, you may then load your mat onto the Cricut machine. You will notice that your machine will begin to detect your scoring tool, as well as your Cricut pen, and will then begin writing your message.

After the machine has written the message you have typed, your Cricut machine will indicate that you must switch out your scoring tool to your fine-point blade, to begin cutting out the card. At this time, you may also remove the pen. That way, there won't be any accidents of unwanted ink spilling onto your card. Once your blade has been secured onto your Cricut machine, you may then begin the cutting process. Your machine will then begin cutting the outline of your card, or if you made two cards on the same, it will begin cutting both. Once your machine has finished cutting your cards, you can unload your mat. The trick to getting the card off of your mat without the card curling is to kind of bend the mat, and just kind of let it peel off on its own. If you do this, your card won't be as bent, as if you were to forcefully peel the card off of the mat. Be very careful not overbend your mat, because it can easily break. If you have decided to use two different colors, you will repeat the writing and cutting process for the second card stock. You will also be doing the same process for any images that you are cutting out as well; however, if you are using multiple colors for an image, you will need to have multiple card stocks in those colors for your Cricut machine to cut out those specific pieces of the image.

Once you have everything cut out, you will begin the gluing process. Glue dots, as well as glue tape, will allow for a clean finish, but a glue stick is more practical and fairly cheap. On your card or cards that were cut out, you will notice the score line that was created. You may fold your cards on this line, and if you have two cards, you may begin gluing these cards together. After assembling all the pieces of your card and gluing them together, you are all set. These cute little cards will be perfect for nearly any occasion, and you can take pride in letting the person receiving the card know that you made it. I'm sure they will be surprised, and it will hold sentimental value, knowing that you took the time to craft this awesome cute card for them.

Making a Re-Usable Stencil on Your Cricut Machine

By now, you are an expert, or, at least, you've boosted your confidence in operating your Cricut machine. But now, you want to be able to create stencils that you can continue to re-use for the long haul.

The following are items that you will need to make your re-usable stencil. You will need a piece of wood, or something that you can paint on. You will need to paint, so any kind of acrylic paint will work just fine. You will need your handy weeding tool and re-positional adhesive spray. Lastly, you will need crafting plastic or transfer sheets. I like to use graphics crafting plastics.

First, you are going to want to open your stencil on your design space. For this stencil that we are making, since we are using crafting plastic, it will not have an adhesive back. So, we will be using our adhesive spray to keep it in place. For my spray, I use Krylon Easy TAC. I've done some research, and found many positive reviews for this spray, which is why I buy it on Amazon.com. You can also find this spray at Michael's.

An important thing to note is, if you are working with any kind of writing, especially in cursive, you are going to want to attach the cutout parts of your letters, so that they stay in your letter. Since you are not working with crafting plastic, these cutouts from your letters will not stick the way they would if you were working with vinyl. To attach the cutouts of your letter to your stencil, what you will need to do, is go to "shapes" on the left side of your screen, and select the square. With this square, you are going to want to make a line shape. This line that you just made can either be thin or thick. You will be moving this line over your letters, to the area that you want your cutouts to be attached to your letters. For example, a cursive letter "e" will have a cutout in the white space. You would then move your line that you created, and attach to your letter "e." You will do this process for any other letters that have similar cutouts. For example, in the word "merry" spelled using cursive, your letters "e," both "r's," and your "y" will have cutouts that need to be attached to your letter. After placing your lines over these letters, you will need to highlight your entire message, and select the weld on the bottom right of your screen. After doing this, the line that you just attached has now become part of the stencil. If you have followed these steps, you will see that all your letters are connected to your stencil. After doing this process, you can now click "make it" on your design space.

We want to make sure that our Cricut machine is set with the proper settings. The setting that I normally cut on is "poster board plus". So, you're going to want to set it onto the little dot after the words "poster board". This setting will make sure that it cuts through the plastic. Before cutting, you are going to want to change your blade to a deep cutting blade, which will be loaded into your clamp B. Next, you can then load your mat and begin to cut. After your Cricut has finished cutting, you can unload your mat and begin the weeding process. After peeling your stencil off of your mat, it is ready to use. For the next portion, you will be needing your paintbrushes as well as your scrap piece of wood, or something to paint on.

You are going to be using your Krylon Easy TAC as well, to help keep your stencil in place, and to prevent it from moving while you are painting. We want our stencil to be sticky, but we don't want it to be permanent to the point where the stencil is too removed. So, you want to make sure that you get the re-positional TAC adhesive. This adhesive will allow you to have just the right amount of hold when painting, and will also let you remove it as well. There are a few tricks to using this adhesive. You are going to want to spray very lightly, because you don't want it to be so sticky that it leaves a sticky residue on your wood or whatever surface that you are working on. After giving it a light mist, you will let your stencil dry for about sixty seconds.

Before sticking your stencil onto a finished piece of wood, you are going to want to try it out on a surface to make sure that it doesn't leave behind a sticky residue when peeling the stencil off. You may notice that, on the first piece of material that you stick your stencil on, there may be some sticky residue that is left behind. So, I would recommend sticking your stencil onto something that you are not going to use to remove the excess residue that may come from your stencil. You can repeat this step multiple times just to ensure that you have the right amount of hold on your stencil.

Now, you may grab the piece of wood that you will be testing your stencil on to see whether or not you like how the stencil looks, and if it will be a keeper. Get your paint ready and start painting over your stencil. If you are using a foam brush, you are going to want to dab your paint onto your stencil, rather than stroking your brush in it. The reason being that, as we are not working on vinyl, your foam brush may get caught on the corners of your plastic stencil. What you can do is, like a dab and small brush combo, just be extra cautious around the corners. After going over your stencil with paint, you can now remove your stencil. If all goes well, your design will come out perfect.

With a small brush, you may now begin touching up your design. For example, where you welded the straight line on your lettering, you will notice that you have areas where paint won't transfer due to the stencil. You can use your small tip brush to connect your lines.

This process will apply to any image that you plan on making a reusable stencil. I mainly refer to writing stencils, because it is a bit easier to explain, since I cannot physically show you what I am referring to.

You might be thinking that this is a lot of work for one stencil, but you have to keep in mind that, after you make this stencil, you are going to be able to keep using this stencil for a very long time. I have many friends that make tons of re-usable stencils, because they sell a lot of the products that they make. I'm sure you can imagine, if you had to make the same stencil over ten times, it would drive you crazy. But, with this stencil, you can easily pump out ten wood designs in about an hour. Eventually, you will have multiple stencils that you can have at your disposal. I highly recommend you give this idea a try.

Conclusion

I am beyond happy that you have made it through this short book. For those of you who had some experience using the Cricut machine, I hope you were able to learn something new or useful. Although the projects are fairly simple, I know that many of the concepts can be carried over to other project ideas as well. For my first-time users, I hope that this book inspired as well as motivated you to learn how to use your Cricut machine to create amazing projects. Again, I would highly recommend that you do more research on Google or YouTube to find more hands-on demonstrations on how to use your Cricut machines, as well as more projects. This was one of the ways that I learnt how my Cricut machine functioned. If there is a project that you read from this book that you are considering in making, I encourage you to type in the title of the project from this book into YouTube. There, you will be able to follow the steps that I have listed in this book as well as any other suggestions that the video may have to offer. Thank you so much, crafters.

Manufactured by Amazon.ca
Bolton, ON

27425962R00042